STRONGER
ME 3
PERSONAL GROWTH JOURNAL

©2020 Current Family, Inc.
www.KUEST.org
All Rights Reserved

ISBN: 978-1-950616-19-0

STRONGER ME

Growing in Spiritual
MATURITY & ENGAGEMENT

As a KUEST Student Leader, you are familiar with the

KUEST CODE

1 Timothy 4:12

*Don't let anyone think less of you because you
are young. Be an example to all believers in word,
in conduct, in love, in spirit, in faith, in purity.*

This is the foundation of being a great leader. In the verses that follow, Paul continues to give Timothy specific instruction for how to become this strong leader:

1 Timothy 4:13-16

[13] Until I get there, focus on reading the Scriptures to the church, encouraging the believers, and teaching them.

[14] Do not neglect the spiritual gift you received through the prophecy spoken over you when the elders of the church laid their hands on you.

[15] Give your complete attention to these matters. Throw yourself into your tasks so that everyone will see your progress.

[16] Keep a close watch on how you live and on your teaching. Stay true to what is right for the sake of your own salvation and the salvation of those who hear you.

All of these instructions fall into two categories: Becoming more spiritually mature, and becoming more engaged in doing the work of ministry. It is from these scriptures that we receive the goal of becoming stronger in Maturity and Engagement, or STRONGER M.E.

A MORE MATURE AND ENGAGED YOU
IS A STRONGER YOU!

We have designed this journal to specifically help you grow in these two areas. Through daily study of the Word and ideas, through the memorizing of key scriptures and through the discipline of reflecting and writing your thoughts, you will grow. You will become more spiritually mature. You will grow in using your gifts and engaging in the work of ministry. So come on, let's get started, we believe you are ready to become a...

WEEK #1
◯ **DAY 1**

Read the principle and the scriptures below. These are the ideas you want to have strong in your heart. Take your time and think about what you are reading. When you have finished this page, place a checkmark next to DAY 1.

PRINCIPLE
I OWN MY DECISIONS

Every day you wake up there are choices to make. From breakfast foods, clothes options, your attitude and the words you choose; to how you treat others and how you choose to cooperate with your parents, the choices are yours. While family, friends and media can influence you and sometimes even cause pressure, the truth is that you completely own every decision you make. You—and only you—own each decision and, as a result, set yourself up for either good or trouble. You can make great choices that lead you into God's Best.

SCRIPTURES
Growing in your knowledge of the Word.

☐ Get wisdom; develop good judgment. Don't forget my words or turn away from them. Proverbs 4:5 NLT

☐ For the Lord gives wisdom; from His mouth comes knowledge and understanding. Proverbs 2:6 NLT

☐ In all your ways acknowledge Him, and He will make your paths straight. Proverbs 3:5 NLT

Place a check-mark next to the scripture you plan to memorize this week. Once you have recited it to a parent or leader, write the scripture in the appropriate box on your Memorized Word page.

4

STRONGER HEART

For the next three days, you will read the lesson below. For each day you will mark the part of the lesson that stands out to you on that day. Each day requires you to use a different method. When you have completed marking the lesson for that day, checkmark the circle.

○DAY 2 | <u>Underline</u>   ○DAY 3 | ⟨Circle⟩   ○DAY 4 | [Bracket]

WISDOM IS SHOUTING

Wouldn't it be amazing if you knew what to do in every situation? Imagine having someone who always knew the right way to go, the right thing to say, the right content to study before a test, the right people to choose as close friends - with you all the time, helping you make great decisions! The truth is, you do! God's Spirit that lives in you is full of God's Wisdom. And, the Bible tells us that this Wisdom is always trying to help direct us. Sometimes this Wisdom is obvious to us, like it is shouting! Sometimes Wisdom is the soft tapping of your conscience, trying to persuade you to do the right thing. We have all felt the tug-of-war on the inside when trying to choose between something we know is right and wrong. You have the opportunity to follow Wisdom's suggestion in every decision that you make. God will never force you to make a decision; He gave you 100% power to own your choices. And, every choice you make has consequences. When you don't listen to Wisdom, it will cost you. But when you follow Wisdom, your choices will lead you to God's best!

WHAT YOU LEARNED ◯ DAY 5

Did you learn more about God's Love or God's Plan? Maybe you learned more about His Character or Truth. Place a checkmark in the box next to what you feel you learned about God. Then take a minute to write what you learned.

◯ **GOD'S LOVE**

◯ **GOD'S CHARACTER**

◯ **GOD'S TRUTH**

◯ **GOD'S PLAN**

Finish these final steps for today's journal. Checkmark each completed task.

◯ **HOW DO YOU PLAN TO MAKE THIS A PART OF YOUR EVERY DAY LIFE?**
[Write your answer in the appropriate **MY PLAN** Box in the back of this journal]

◯ **WHAT IS ONE POTENTIAL AREA OF WEAKNESS YOU WILL ASK THE HOLY SPIRIT TO HELP YOU MAKE STRONGER?**

[Stop now and ask the Holy Spirit for help in this area]

◯ **ENCOURAGE A FRIEND**
[Share empowering thoughts, ideas, words, and scriptures with your friends. Know what's going on in your friends lives. Make those things a matter of prayer. Find and share scriptures to encourage them.]

THE NAME OF THE FRIEND YOU ENCOURAGED:

THIS IS WHAT I DID: [circle all that you did]

called them   texted them   emailed them   talked to them   wrote a letter

6

MY PERSONAL
NOTES

Read the principle and the scriptures below. These are the ideas you want to have strong in your heart. Take your time and think about what you are reading. When you have finished this page, place a checkmark next to DAY 1.

PRINCIPLE

IF IT'S TOUGH ON ME, IT'S BUILDING TOUGH IN ME

A disciplined lifestyle of lifting weights and putting yourself through strenuous physical exercise feels tough. It makes you sweat. It causes your muscles to be so sore that sometimes you can hardly walk! It takes commitment and time and giving up being lazy. It feels tough, but there are definitely rewards: a tough, physically fit, strong body that can even increase your health so you will live longer! When we experience tough things, it builds tough in us. When we stick with tough things, we grow and develop great skills and it leads us to great rewards!

SCRIPTURES

Growing in your knowledge of the Word.

☐ I can do all things through Christ who strengthens me. Philippians 4:13 NKJV

☐ For when I am weak, then I am strong. 2 Corinthians 9:11 NKJV

☐ But the Helper, the Holy Spirit, whom the Father will send in My name, He will teach you all things, and bring to your remembrance all things that I said to you. John 14:26 NKJV

Place a check-mark next to the scripture you plan to memorize this week. Once you have recited it to a parent or leader, write the scripture in the appropriate box on your Memorized Word page.

8

For the next three days, you will read the lesson below. For each day you will mark the part of the lesson that stands out to you on that day. Each day requires you to use a different method. When you have completed marking the lesson for that day, checkmark the circle.

○DAY 2 | Underline   ○DAY 3 | Circle   ○DAY 4 | [Bracket]

I HAVE GRIT

In life, we will go through some hard things. Some of these difficult things we choose, like pushing ourselves with more lessons or practice time in order to increase our skill level and sharpen a talent. Sometimes, the hard things we must walk through we don't choose at all! They seem unfair, like experiencing the death of someone you love or being betrayed or even mistreated. At times, we may experience an epic fail, and it can be really hard to get past the shame of the mistake, to get up and to grow past it. But you know what? Whenever you face something tough, you can make it through that hard thing. Why? Because inside you have GRIT. You have what it takes to face the adversity because you are full of courage, persistence, and the ability to bounce back. As a leader, you don't shy away from hard things. You don't run from difficulty. You never assume things are impossible. You are able to face the them, deal with them, and exercise your strength to get past them. You are not alone in this. God's Spirit in you will give you power and teach you how to overcome any difficulty.

WHAT YOU LEARNED ○ DAY 5

Did you learn more about God's Love or God's Plan? Maybe you learned more about His Character or Truth. Place a checkmark in the box next to what you feel you learned about God. Then take a minute to write what you learned.

○ **GOD'S LOVE**

○ **GOD'S CHARACTER**

○ **GOD'S TRUTH**

○ **GOD'S PLAN**

Finish these final steps for today's journal. Checkmark each completed task.

○ **HOW DO YOU PLAN TO MAKE THIS A PART OF YOUR EVERY DAY LIFE?**

[Write your answer in the appropriate **MY PLAN** Box in the back of this journal]

○ **WHAT IS ONE POTENTIAL AREA OF WEAKNESS YOU WILL ASK THE HOLY SPIRIT TO HELP YOU MAKE STRONGER?**

[Stop now and ask the Holy Spirit for help in this area]

○ **ENCOURAGE A FRIEND**

[Share empowering thoughts, ideas, words, and scriptures with your friends. Know what's going on in your friends lives. Make those things a matter of prayer. Find and share scriptures to encourage them.]

THE NAME OF THE FRIEND YOU ENCOURAGED:

THIS IS WHAT I DID: [circle all that you did]

called them   texted them   emailed them   talked to them   wrote a letter

10

MY PERSONAL NOTES

WEEK #3
⭕ DAY 1

Read the principle and the scriptures below. These are the ideas you want to have strong in your heart. Take your time and think about what you are reading. When you have finished this page, place a checkmark next to DAY 1.

PRINCIPLE

I CONTROL THE STRENGTH OF MY MUSCLES

Have you ever seen "before and after" pictures of body builders? It's amazing that a person who appears to have a normal body, or even one that is flabby or out-of-shape, can turn into someone that looks like the Incredible Hulk! How is that possible? A decision, a plan, a good coach and the discipline to follow the plan. Each of us controls the strength of our muscles. How strong and fit do you want to be physically? How strong and fit do you want to be spiritually? You have complete control.

SCRIPTURES
Growing in your knowledge of the Word.

☐ I discipline my body like an athlete, training it to do what it should. 1 Corinthians 9:26 NLT

☐ For the Spirit God gave us does not make us timid, but gives us power, love and self-discipline. 2 Timothy 1:7 NIV

☐ But you, take courage! Do not let your hands be weak, for your work shall be rewarded." 2 Chronicles 15:7 ESV

Place a check-mark next to the scripture you plan to memorize this week. Once you have recited it to a parent or leader, write the scripture in the appropriate box on your Memorized Word page.

12

◯ DAYS 2-4

STRONGER HEART

For the next three days, you will read the lesson below. For each day you will mark the part of the lesson that stands out to you on that day. Each day requires you to use a different method. When you have completed marking the lesson for that day, checkmark the circle.

◯ **DAY 2 | <u>Underline</u>**   ◯ **DAY 3 | (Circle)**   ◯ **DAY 4 | [Bracket]**

MY CHOICES BUILD—OR LIMIT—MY STRENGTH

Your strength is determined by your choices. We can easily tell if a person lifts weights because their physical muscles prove it. But what about the muscles on the inside? Mental muscles like knowledge, critical thinking and mental toughness? Soul muscles like love, kindness, courage, confidence and self-esteem? Or spiritual muscles like faith and authority? Your strength in all of these areas - whether muscles in your physical body, your brain, your soul or your spirit – is a direct result of how you work your muscles. What you put into them, and how you exercise your muscles determine how strong or how weak you are. Your choices either build strength or limit strength. The good news is, when you discover an area where you feel weak (maybe your arms, the math-skill section of your brain, your ability to forgive, or your self-esteem), you have the ability to strengthen this part of you. A trusted mentor, coach or teacher can help connect you to what you need to strengthen your muscles, like scriptures, podcasts, tutoring, or physical exercises. You determine your strength – so be strong in every way!

13

WHAT YOU LEARNED ⃝DAY 5

Did you learn more about God's Love or God's Plan? Maybe you learned more about His Character or Truth. Place a checkmark in the box next to what you feel you learned about God. Then take a minute to write what you learned.

⃝ **GOD'S LOVE**

⃝ **GOD'S CHARACTER**

⃝ **GOD'S TRUTH**

⃝ **GOD'S PLAN**

Finish these final steps for today's journal. Checkmark each completed task.

⃝ **HOW DO YOU PLAN TO MAKE THIS A PART OF YOUR EVERY DAY LIFE?**
[Write your answer in the appropriate **MY PLAN** Box in the back of this journal]

⃝ **WHAT IS ONE POTENTIAL AREA OF WEAKNESS YOU WILL ASK THE HOLY SPIRIT TO HELP YOU MAKE STRONGER?**

[Stop now and ask the Holy Spirit for help in this area]

⃝ **ENCOURAGE A FRIEND**
[Share empowering thoughts, ideas, words, and scriptures with your friends. Know what's going on in your friends lives. Make those things a matter of prayer. Find and share scriptures to encourage them.]

THE NAME OF THE FRIEND YOU ENCOURAGED:

THIS IS WHAT I DID: [circle all that you did]

called them   texted them   emailed them   talked to them   wrote a letter

14

MY PERSONAL
NOTES

Read the principle and the scriptures below. These are the ideas you want to have strong in your heart. Take your time and think about what you are reading. When you have finished this page, place a checkmark next to DAY 1.

PRINCIPLE

I OWN MY INTEGRITY

Integrity is developed over time as you do the right thing over and over, even when no one is watching. Of course, we know that God is always watching; He sees your actions, your motives and your most secret thoughts. Integrity means you make choices that are honest, and your decisions are moral and ethical. As a person of integrity, you are consistent and trustworthy. You act the same in front of your parents as you do with your friends. Because you live with integrity, you do the right thing, every time, no matter who you are with.

SCRIPTURES
Growing in your knowledge of the Word.

☐ When the Spirit of truth comes, he will guide you into all truth. John 16:13 NLT

☐ The integrity of the upright guides them, but the unfaithful are destroyed by their duplicity. Proverbs 11:3 NIV

☐ To do what is right and just is more acceptable to the Lord than sacrifice. Proverbs 21:3 NIV

Place a check-mark next to the scripture you plan to memorize this week. Once you have recited it to a parent or leader, write the scripture in the appropriate box on your Memorized Word page.

16

For the next three days, you will read the lesson below. For each day you will mark the part of the lesson that stands out to you on that day. Each day requires you to use a different method. When you have completed marking the lesson for that day, checkmark the circle.

◯ DAY 2 | Underline   ◯ DAY 3 | Circle   ◯ DAY 4 | [Bracket]

IT'S UP TO ME TO DO THE RIGHT THING

Did you hear the amazing story about the family driving down a country road, who discovered large trash bags in the middle of the street? Believing they were litter, they put the bags in their vehicle. Hours later, they discovered the bags were filled with dollars. Lots of dollars – nearly one million of them! They immediately called the local sheriff's office to turn them in. The mother said turning over the cash was a no-brainer; it was the right thing to do since the money didn't belong to them.

How easy would it be for you to return all this cash that you found, fair and square? Some people may think, "I deserve to keep it!" But what about you? Doing the right thing, even if many people may not, is the clear choice when you operate in integrity. It's up to you to do the right thing, every time and in every choice, when the right thing seems easy and when it seems hard. You can make the right decisions because you have God's Spirit in you. God's Spirit always leads to Truth, pointing to what is right. You can walk in integrity and do the right thing!

WHAT YOU LEARNED ○ DAY 5

Did you learn more about God's Love or God's Plan? Maybe you learned more about His Character or Truth. Place a checkmark in the box next to what you feel you learned about God. Then take a minute to write what you learned.

○ **GOD'S LOVE**

○ **GOD'S CHARACTER**

○ **GOD'S TRUTH**

○ **GOD'S PLAN**

Finish these final steps for today's journal. Checkmark each completed task.

○ **HOW DO YOU PLAN TO MAKE THIS A PART OF YOUR EVERY DAY LIFE?**

[Write your answer in the appropriate **MY PLAN** Box in the back of this journal]

○ **WHAT IS ONE POTENTIAL AREA OF WEAKNESS YOU WILL ASK THE HOLY SPIRIT TO HELP YOU MAKE STRONGER?**

[Stop now and ask the Holy Spirit for help in this area]

○ **ENCOURAGE A FRIEND**

[Share empowering thoughts, ideas, words, and scriptures with your friends. Know what's going on in your friends lives. Make those things a matter of prayer. Find and share scriptures to encourage them.]

THE NAME OF THE FRIEND YOU ENCOURAGED:

THIS IS WHAT I DID: [circle all that you did]

called them   texted them   emailed them   talked to them   wrote a letter

18

MY PERSONAL NOTES

Read the principle and the scriptures below. These are the ideas you want to have strong in your heart. Take your time and think about what you are reading. When you have finished this page, place a checkmark next to DAY 1.

PRINCIPLE

I RESPOND TO TRUTH, AND REJECT LIES

"The Spirit shows what is true and will come and guide you into the full truth..." John 16:13. You have an Internal Truth Detector inside you! He helps you detect and understand what is right and true, keeping you from being tricked to believe lies. Our culture is full of half-truths, little white lies, and big, fat lies. Just for the record, ALL lies are harmful and lies are how the enemy tries to trick us to believe and do things that will cause us harm. But you can respond to Truth and reject lies!

SCRIPTURES

Growing in your knowledge of the Word.

☐ The Spirit shows what is true and will come and guide you into the full truth..." John 16:13 CEV

☐ Stay alert! Watch out for your great enemy, the devil. He prowls around like a roaring lion, looking for someone to devour. 1 Peter 5:8 NLT

☐ You will open their eyes and turn them from darkness to light and from Satan's control to God's. Acts 26:18 GWT

Place a check-mark next to the scripture you plan to memorize this week. Once you have recited it to a parent or leader, write the scripture in the appropriate box on your Memorized Word page.

20

For the next three days, you will read the lesson below. For each day you will mark the part of the lesson that stands out to you on that day. Each day requires you to use a different method. When you have completed marking the lesson for that day, checkmark the circle.

○ DAY 2 | <u>Underline</u>   ○ DAY 3 | (Circle)   ○ DAY 4 | [Bracket]

I'M NOT SPIDER BAIT!

Have you ever been walking along outside, enjoying a great day, and then walk right through a spider web that sticks to you everywhere? Its creepy! It's amazing how quickly a web can be created, and how cleverly it's crafted! There are tiny strings that are almost invisible, weaving in and out of each other in such a way that it creates a trap. When insects get caught in this trap, they meet their fate and are devoured by the crafty spider. Just like these insects, we have to be on the lookout for clever webs of deceit. Our enemy is constantly trying to deceive us, trying to persuade us to believe something misleading, dishonest, or false. He takes truth and twists it just enough for it to seem right. Our culture is so entangled in webs of deceit. Everything can seem fine but watch out! When you are deceived, it's like getting stuck in a webby trap to be devoured! But you can keep from being tricked! Gods spirit in you helps you know Truth. You can steer clear of webs of deceit and stay safe from being devoured!

WHAT YOU LEARNED ⃝ DAY 5

Did you learn more about God's Love or God's Plan? Maybe you learned more about His Character or Truth. Place a checkmark in the box next to what you feel you learned about God. Then take a minute to write what you learned.

⃝ **GOD'S LOVE**

⃝ **GOD'S CHARACTER**

⃝ **GOD'S TRUTH**

⃝ **GOD'S PLAN**

Finish these final steps for today's journal. Checkmark each completed task.

⃝ **HOW DO YOU PLAN TO MAKE THIS A PART OF YOUR EVERY DAY LIFE?**
[Write your answer in the appropriate **MY PLAN** Box in the back of this journal]

⃝ **WHAT IS ONE POTENTIAL AREA OF WEAKNESS YOU WILL ASK THE HOLY SPIRIT TO HELP YOU MAKE STRONGER?**

[Stop now and ask the Holy Spirit for help in this area]

⃝ **ENCOURAGE A FRIEND**
[Share empowering thoughts, ideas, words, and scriptures with your friends. Know what's going on in your friends lives. Make those things a matter of prayer. Find and share scriptures to encourage them.]

THE NAME OF THE FRIEND YOU ENCOURAGED:

THIS IS WHAT I DID: [circle all that you did]

called them   texted them   emailed them   talked to them   wrote a letter

22

MY PERSONAL NOTES

Read the principle and the scriptures below. These are the ideas you want to have strong in your heart. Take your time and think about what you are reading. When you have finished this page, place a checkmark next to DAY 1.

PRINCIPLE

I STAND AT THE GATE

Your eyes and ears are like gates into your mind. What you allow yourself to see and hear influences you, and greatly affects your life. If we watch scary movies, that will affect us by causing fear. If we listen to sad music constantly, it will stir up sadness. If we read self-help books, we will be motivated to grow ourselves and become strong. Whatever you see and hear really does impact your thoughts, feelings and actions. You are the only one who stands at the gate of your mind, and you have the power to choose what gets in.

SCRIPTURES
Growing in your knowledge of the Word.

☐ The eye is the lamp of the body. So, if your eye is healthy, your whole body will be full of light, but if your eye is bad, your whole body will be full of darkness. Matthew 6:22-23 ESV

☐ Set your gaze on the path before you. With fixed purpose, looking straight ahead, *ignore life's distractions.* Proverbs 4:25 TPT

☐ Open my eyes to see the wonderful truths in your instructions. Psalm 119:18 NLT

Place a check-mark next to the scripture you plan to memorize this week. Once you have recited it to a parent or leader, write the scripture in the appropriate box on your Memorized Word page.

24

○ DAYS 2-4

STRONGER HEART

For the next three days, you will read the lesson below. For each day you will mark the part of the lesson that stands out to you on that day. Each day requires you to use a different method. When you have completed marking the lesson for that day, checkmark the circle.

○ DAY 2 | Underline   ○ DAY 3 | Circle   ○ DAY 4 | [Bracket]

THE BLAME GAME

If you have ever received a low grade because you didn't study for a test, it's a pretty bad feeling. If you've ever let words fly out of your mouth that hurt someone, that feels pretty lousy too. A lot of times, when we make a mistake or we find ourselves in a sticky situation, our human response is to look for someone or something to blame. It's human nature to enter the blame game to make us feel better. The blame game is something everyone has played. The truth, however, is that there is really no one else to blame for our mistakes. We think and act because of what we see and hear. Every word we speak and everything we do is a result of what we have allowed into our minds to shape our thoughts and actions. So if we allow ourselves to be lazy, act unkindly, or be selfish, there is no one else to blame. We alone are responsible for what we say and how we act.

25

WHAT YOU LEARNED ○ DAY 5

Did you learn more about God's Love or God's Plan? Maybe you learned more about His Character or Truth. Place a checkmark in the box next to what you feel you learned about God. Then take a minute to write what you learned.

○ **GOD'S LOVE**

○ **GOD'S CHARACTER**

○ **GOD'S TRUTH**

○ **GOD'S PLAN**

Finish these final steps for today's journal. Checkmark each completed task.

○ **HOW DO YOU PLAN TO MAKE THIS A PART OF YOUR EVERY DAY LIFE?**
[Write your answer in the appropriate **MY PLAN** Box in the back of this journal]

○ **WHAT IS ONE POTENTIAL AREA OF WEAKNESS YOU WILL ASK THE HOLY SPIRIT TO HELP YOU MAKE STRONGER?**

[Stop now and ask the Holy Spirit for help in this area]

○ **ENCOURAGE A FRIEND**
[Share empowering thoughts, ideas, words, and scriptures with your friends. Know what's going on in your friends lives. Make those things a matter of prayer. Find and share scriptures to encourage them.]

THE NAME OF THE FRIEND YOU ENCOURAGED:

THIS IS WHAT I DID: [circle all that you did]

called them   texted them   emailed them   talked to them   wrote a letter

26

MY PERSONAL
NOTES

Read the principle and the scriptures below. These are the ideas you want to have strong in your heart. Take your time and think about what you are reading. When you have finished this page, place a checkmark next to DAY 1.

PRINCIPLE

I HAVE WHAT IT TAKES TO SERVE

Which are you: the one who takes on your assigned tasks quickly, or the one who procrastinates and dreads tasks until the last minute? Do you know that you have the power to serve promptly AND with a great attitude? It's your choice, and you have what it takes to serve well!

SCRIPTURES
Growing in your knowledge of the Word.

☐ Yet it shall not be so among you; but whoever desires to become great among you, let him be your servant. Matthew 20:26 NKJV

☐ And never let ugly or hateful words come from your mouth, but instead let your words become beautiful gifts that encourage others; do this by speaking words of grace to help them. Ephesians 4:29 TPT

☐ Work willingly at whatever you do, as though you were working for the Lord rather than for people. Colossians 3:23 NLT

Place a check-mark next to the scripture you plan to memorize this week. Once you have recited it to a parent or leader, write the scripture in the appropriate box on your Memorized Word page.

28

◯ DAYS 2-4

STRONGER HEART

For the next three days, you will read the lesson below. For each day you will mark the part of the lesson that stands out to you on that day. Each day requires you to use a different method. When you have completed marking the lesson for that day, checkmark the circle.

◯DAY 2 | <u>Underline</u>   ◯DAY 3 | (Circle)   ◯DAY 4 | [Bracket]

MY PLEASURE

Have you ever encountered a super pleasant, energetic person waiting on you at a restaurant or hotel? Wow! Their smile, positive vibe, and "no-problem" enthusiasm goes a long way as they help you and brighten your day. On the other hand, have you experienced someone serving you with a terrible attitude? Yikes! Their poor attitude can actually ruin a great dinner or experience. When you are serving at home, at a job or at church, how can you make sure that your attitude is pleasant? How would you describe the kind of attitude you would like to have serving? Displaying energy, kindness, and great manners, engaging those you are serving, complimenting others, and even just smiling, are great traits that exude an amazing attitude! You can choose to serve excellently and brighten the day of those that you serve!

www.KUEST.org

WHAT YOU LEARNED ◯ DAY 5

Did you learn more about God's Love or God's Plan? Maybe you learned more about His Character or Truth. Place a checkmark in the box next to what you feel you learned about God. Then take a minute to write what you learned.

◯ **GOD'S LOVE**

◯ **GOD'S CHARACTER**

◯ **GOD'S TRUTH**

◯ **GOD'S PLAN**

Finish these final steps for today's journal. Checkmark each completed task.

◯ **HOW DO YOU PLAN TO MAKE THIS A PART OF YOUR EVERY DAY LIFE?**
[Write your answer in the appropriate **MY PLAN** Box in the back of this journal]

◯ **WHAT IS ONE POTENTIAL AREA OF WEAKNESS YOU WILL ASK THE HOLY SPIRIT TO HELP YOU MAKE STRONGER?**

[Stop now and ask the Holy Spirit for help in this area]

◯ **ENCOURAGE A FRIEND**
[Share empowering thoughts, ideas, words, and scriptures with your friends. Know what's going on in your friends lives. Make those things a matter of prayer. Find and share scriptures to encourage them.]

THE NAME OF THE FRIEND YOU ENCOURAGED:

THIS IS WHAT I DID: [circle all that you did]

called them   texted them   emailed them   talked to them   wrote a letter

30

MY PERSONAL NOTES

Read the principle and the scriptures below. These are the ideas you want to have strong in your heart. Take your time and think about what you are reading. When you have finished this page, place a checkmark next to DAY 1.

PRINCIPLE

YOU CAN'T FAKE IT AND MAKE IT

It's cleaning day, so you head to your room and do everything, but clean! You get distracted, and then later, when your parent checks in, you act like you've been cleaning the entire time! Sound familiar? We've probably all done this! But trying to fake others causes you to miss the mark. Pretending to work hard will never help you, but it will put you behind and can actually bring trouble into your life. You always know if you are giving your best or if you are faking it. So be honest, don't fake it, and work hard!

SCRIPTURES

Growing in your knowledge of the Word.

☐ And I praise you because of the wonderful way you created me. Everything you do is marvelous! Of this I have no doubt. Psalm 139:14 CEV

☐ You saw me before I was born. Every day of my life was recorded in your book. Every moment was laid out before a single day had passed. Psalm 139:16 NLT

☐ Examine yourselves to see if your faith is genuine. Test yourselves. Surely you know that Jesus Christ is among you; if not, you have failed the test of genuine faith. 2 Cor 13:5 NLT

Place a check-mark next to the scripture you plan to memorize this week. Once you have recited it to a parent or leader, write the scripture in the appropriate box on your Memorized Word page.

STRONGER HEART

For the next three days, you will read the lesson below. For each day you will mark the part of the lesson that stands out to you on that day. Each day requires you to use a different method. When you have completed marking the lesson for that day, checkmark the circle.

◯DAY 2 | <u>Underline</u>   ◯DAY 3 | Ⓒircle   ◯DAY 4 | [Bracket]

THE REAL DEAL

The pressure to fit in. It's pretty intense in middle school and junior high. There is so much pressure to be like someone else. Have you ever felt that way? Here's some good news: God didn't design you to look like everyone else, act like everyone else, and try to be like everyone else. Don't be pressured to perform or be fake. Be the real you because you are the Real Deal! When God created you, He wasn't hoping you would try to be like someone else. His thoughts were probably something like, "I hope that they understand how incredible they are. I hope that they take all the giftings, great character, and amazingness I put into them and be who I've created them to be!" Anytime we try to hide who we are or try to be someone else, we are not being genuine. We are actually devaluing the gift we really are and making less of who God created us to be! When we recognize that we have great value and worth in God's eyes, it frees us to be genuinely us! So be the Real Deal- to yourself, to God and to the world around you!

WHAT YOU LEARNED ○ DAY 5

Did you learn more about God's Love or God's Plan? Maybe you learned more about His Character or Truth. Place a checkmark in the box next to what you feel you learned about God. Then take a minute to write what you learned.

○ **GOD'S LOVE**

○ **GOD'S CHARACTER**

○ **GOD'S TRUTH**

○ **GOD'S PLAN**

Finish these final steps for today's journal. Checkmark each completed task.

○ **HOW DO YOU PLAN TO MAKE THIS A PART OF YOUR EVERY DAY LIFE?**
[Write your answer in the appropriate **MY PLAN** Box in the back of this journal]

○ **WHAT IS ONE POTENTIAL AREA OF WEAKNESS YOU WILL ASK THE HOLY SPIRIT TO HELP YOU MAKE STRONGER?**

[Stop now and ask the Holy Spirit for help in this area]

○ **ENCOURAGE A FRIEND**
[Share empowering thoughts, ideas, words, and scriptures with your friends. Know what's going on in your friends lives. Make those things a matter of prayer. Find and share scriptures to encourage them.]

THE NAME OF THE FRIEND YOU ENCOURAGED:

THIS IS WHAT I DID: [circle all that you did]

called them   texted them   emailed them   talked to them   wrote a letter

MY PERSONAL NOTES

Read the principle and the scriptures below. These are the ideas you want to have strong in your heart. Take your time and think about what you are reading. When you have finished this page, place a checkmark next to DAY 1.

PRINCIPLE

IT STARTS WITH "I"

Yes, the word "it" starts with an "i," but the word we are really talking about here is "initiative". Initiative is when you motivate yourself to get something going. Initiative is when "I" choose to start. Initiative is when "I" do what is necessary without anyone else telling me. "I" have the ability to motivate myself and get stuff done! "I" have initiative!

SCRIPTURES
Growing in your knowledge of the Word.

☐ Lazy people are soon poor; hard workers get rich. Proverbs 10:4 NLT

☐ Diligent hands will rule, but laziness ends in forced labor. Proverbs 12:24 NIV

☐ Good planning and hard work lead to prosperity, but hasty shortcuts lead to poverty. Proverbs 21:5 NLT

Place a check-mark next to the scripture you plan to memorize this week. Once you have recited it to a parent or leader, write the scripture in the appropriate box on your Memorized Word page.

36

For the next three days, you will read the lesson below. For each day you will mark the part of the lesson that stands out to you on that day. Each day requires you to use a different method. When you have completed marking the lesson for that day, checkmark the circle.

○ DAY 2 | <u>Underline</u>   ○ DAY 3 | (Circle)   ○ DAY 4 | [Bracket]

I DO THINGS WITHOUT BEING TOLD

When you were younger, you may remember your parents reminding you to say "please" or to say "thank you". Even now, you can probably think of times when you are reminded to "turn out the lights"… "put on sunscreen"… "clean your room"… "do your schoolwork". Most students don't like being reminded to do things. Some days, it can seem frustrating and can make you feel like a kindergartener! So how can you escape all the reminders? Easy – take initiative! Do things without being told! If your parent came home to a room that was organized and clean (not just everything shoved under the bed, but really clean!), would they faint? If you actually DID the things you know you should do at home and with your schoolwork, if you developed a pattern of just getting things done, before long, they would no longer need to remind you! You are a leader. This starts with leading yourself. So take initiative. Do things without being told!

WHAT YOU LEARNED ○ DAY 5

Did you learn more about God's Love or God's Plan? Maybe you learned more about His Character or Truth. Place a checkmark in the box next to what you feel you learned about God. Then take a minute to write what you learned.

○ **GOD'S LOVE**

○ **GOD'S CHARACTER**

○ **GOD'S TRUTH**

○ **GOD'S PLAN**

Finish these final steps for today's journal. Checkmark each completed task.

● **HOW DO YOU PLAN TO MAKE THIS A PART OF YOUR EVERY DAY LIFE?**
[Write your answer in the appropriate **MY PLAN** Box in the back of this journal]

● **WHAT IS ONE POTENTIAL AREA OF WEAKNESS YOU WILL ASK THE HOLY SPIRIT TO HELP YOU MAKE STRONGER?**

[Stop now and ask the Holy Spirit for help in this area]

● **ENCOURAGE A FRIEND**
[Share empowering thoughts, ideas, words, and scriptures with your friends. Know what's going on in your friends lives. Make those things a matter of prayer. Find and share scriptures to encourage them.]

THE NAME OF THE FRIEND YOU ENCOURAGED:

THIS IS WHAT I DID: [circle all that you did]

called them   texted them   emailed them   talked to them   wrote a letter

38

MY PERSONAL NOTES

Read the principle and the scriptures below. These are the ideas you want to have strong in your heart. Take your time and think about what you are reading. When you have finished this page, place a checkmark next to DAY 1.

PRINCIPLE

HUMILITY IS THE REAL STRENGTH

If someone asked you what it means to be strong, what things come to mind? You might consider things like big muscles, courage, endurance, the ability to lead others. Would humility even cross your mind? Humility is understanding all strength comes from God. Humility is lowering yourself before God, refusing to be arrogant and foolish. When you do this, God gives His power, His wisdom, and His favor. Humility positions us to be the strongest we can be!

SCRIPTURES
Growing in your knowledge of the Word.

☐ God resists the proud, but gives grace to the humble. James 4:6 NKJV

☐ All of you young people should obey your elders. In fact, everyone should be humble toward everyone else. The Scriptures say, "God opposes proud people, but he helps everyone who is humble." 1 Peter 5:5 CEV

☐ Therefore He says: "God resists the proud, But gives grace to the humble." 1 Peter 5:6 NKJV

Place a check-mark next to the scripture you plan to memorize this week. Once you have recited it to a parent or leader, write the scripture in the appropriate box on your Memorized Word page.

40

STRONGER HEART

For the next three days, you will read the lesson below. For each day you will mark the part of the lesson that stands out to you on that day. Each day requires you to use a different method. When you have completed marking the lesson for that day, checkmark the circle.

○DAY 2 | Underline   ○DAY 3 | Circle   ○DAY 4 | [Bracket]

IF I'M HUMBLE, I'M THE FAVORITE!

Did you know that kindness and humility are traits that God chooses to bless? God gives GRACE to the humble, and grace is His favor, power and blessing. And, Proverbs tells us that if we wear loyalty and kindness and God finds them in our heart, then we will find favor with God and people! Do you want to be people's favorite? Do you want to be God's favorite? Live a life of kindness and humility. Many people today think that you have to be a show-off, speak your mind, and bravely tell people what to do in order to be a strong leader. A few people may think that is impressive, but not many, especially God. The way to impress Him and receive His blessing, favor and power is by humbling yourself to Him and being kind to others. That takes self-control. That takes preferring others. That's real strength. That is great leadership!

www.KUEST.org

WHAT YOU LEARNED

◯ DAY 5

Did you learn more about God's Love or God's Plan? Maybe you learned more about His Character or Truth. Place a checkmark in the box next to what you feel you learned about God. Then take a minute to write what you learned.

◯ **GOD'S LOVE**

◯ **GOD'S CHARACTER**

◯ **GOD'S TRUTH**

◯ **GOD'S PLAN**

Finish these final steps for today's journal. Checkmark each completed task.

◯ **HOW DO YOU PLAN TO MAKE THIS A PART OF YOUR EVERY DAY LIFE?**
[Write your answer in the appropriate **MY PLAN** Box in the back of this journal]

◯ **WHAT IS ONE POTENTIAL AREA OF WEAKNESS YOU WILL ASK THE HOLY SPIRIT TO HELP YOU MAKE STRONGER?**

[Stop now and ask the Holy Spirit for help in this area]

◯ **ENCOURAGE A FRIEND**
[Share empowering thoughts, ideas, words, and scriptures with your friends. Know what's going on in your friends lives. Make those things a matter of prayer. Find and share scriptures to encourage them.]

THE NAME OF THE FRIEND YOU ENCOURAGED:

THIS IS WHAT I DID: [circle all that you did]

called them   texted them   emailed them   talked to them   wrote a letter

MY PERSONAL NOTES

Read the principle and the scriptures below. These are the ideas you want to have strong in your heart. Take your time and think about what you are reading. When you have finished this page, place a checkmark next to DAY 1.

PRINCIPLE

I MUST FOLLOW WELL TO LEAD WELL

Do you remember playing, "Follow the Leader?" The winner is the one who best mimics the leader's actions, but the ones who fail to do exactly what the leader does, are out! To be a great leader, you must be a great follower, which requires staying aware, being conscientious, paying attention to everything around you, and humility. As you practice these things, you are developing great leader muscles! Be the best follower to your spiritual leaders and those who are in authority in your life! Follow well so you can lead well!

SCRIPTURES
Growing in your knowledge of the Word.

☐ The student is not above the teacher, nor a servant above his master. Mathew 10:24 NIV

☐ But now the LORD declares: I promise that I will honor those who honor me, and those who despise me will be considered insignificant. 1 Sam 2:30 GWT

☐ If you honor your father and mother, "things will go well for you, and you will have a long life on the earth." Ephesians 6:3 NLT

Place a check-mark next to the scripture you plan to memorize this week. Once you have recited it to a parent or leader, write the scripture in the appropriate box on your Memorized Word page.

For the next three days, you will read the lesson below. For each day you will mark the part of the lesson that stands out to you on that day. Each day requires you to use a different method. When you have completed marking the lesson for that day, checkmark the circle.

○ **DAY 2 | Underline**   ○ **DAY 3 | Circle**   ○ **DAY 4 | [Bracket]**

HONOR BRINGS REWARD

Honor isn't taught very much in our culture today, but The Bible teaches a lot about honor. It is full of examples of people who walked in honor, as well as people who showed dishonor, and what the consequences are of each. Honor means we recognize the importance and the value of someone. We respect them highly and show that we appreciate them. Pause for a minute. Do you treat God like you value Him? Do you treat your parents and grandparents like they are the most important people in your life? Do you value your pastors and teachers? The Bible shows that we should honor all of these people in our lives. When we honor, God rewards us. For instance, when we honor God, He promises to honor us by helping us, giving us favor, and seeing to it that we have good things. When we choose to honor our parents, God promises to reward us with a long life! Just think about that! If you dishonor your parents, you can cut your life short! When you show honor to others by serving them, God promises to promote you. Honor takes humility, and it brings rewards into our lives.

WHAT YOU LEARNED ○ DAY 5

Did you learn more about God's Love or God's Plan? Maybe you learned more about His Character or Truth. Place a checkmark in the box next to what you feel you learned about God. Then take a minute to write what you learned.

○ **GOD'S LOVE**

○ **GOD'S CHARACTER**

○ **GOD'S TRUTH**

○ **GOD'S PLAN**

Finish these final steps for today's journal. Checkmark each completed task.

○ **HOW DO YOU PLAN TO MAKE THIS A PART OF YOUR EVERY DAY LIFE?**
[Write your answer in the appropriate **MY PLAN** Box in the back of this journal]

○ **WHAT IS ONE POTENTIAL AREA OF WEAKNESS YOU WILL ASK THE HOLY SPIRIT TO HELP YOU MAKE STRONGER?**

[Stop now and ask the Holy Spirit for help in this area]

○ **ENCOURAGE A FRIEND**
[Share empowering thoughts, ideas, words, and scriptures with your friends. Know what's going on in your friends lives. Make those things a matter of prayer. Find and share scriptures to encourage them.]

THE NAME OF THE FRIEND YOU ENCOURAGED:

THIS IS WHAT I DID: [circle all that you did]

called them   texted them   emailed them   talked to them   wrote a lette

46

MY PERSONAL
NOTES

Read the principle and the scriptures below. These are the ideas you want to have strong in your heart. Take your time and think about what you are reading. When you have finished this page, place a checkmark next to DAY 1.

PRINCIPLE
I LOOK OVER MY SHOULDER

One rule of great leadership is "looking over your shoulder". For example, when you clean your room, look back over your shoulder before your walk out, to double check everything is done. When you create this habit, it will bring great benefit to you! By "looking over your shoulder," you will double check your math problems, and find the mistakes, resulting in a better grade. You will look again before leaving your lunch in the back seat of the car! You will pay attention to others and notice they need encouragement. "Looking over your shoulder" helps you and others!

SCRIPTURES
Growing in your knowledge of the Word.

☐ But as you excel in everything – in faith, in speech, in knowledge, in all earnestness, and in our love for you – see that you excel in this act of grace also. 2 Corinthians 8:7 ESV

☐ In everything set them an example by doing what is good. Titus 2:7 NIV

☐ Whatever you do, work at it with all your heart, as though you were working for the Lord and not for people. Colossians 3:23 GNT

Place a check-mark next to the scripture you plan to memorize this week. Once you have recited it to a parent or leader, write the scripture in the appropriate box on your Memorized Word page.

For the next three days, you will read the lesson below. For each day you will mark the part of the lesson that stands out to you on that day. Each day requires you to use a different method. When you have completed marking the lesson for that day, checkmark the circle.

○ DAY 2 | <u>Underline</u>　○ DAY 3 | (Circle)　○ DAY 4 | [Bracket]

FOLLOW THROUGH, FOLLOW UP

Do you remember learning the "clean up song" that was made popular by the big, purple dinosaur, Barney? If toys were scattered on the floor, before the episode ended, the cast would all sing the song together as they cleaned up the mess and put everything back in its place. You are way past preschool, but how would you rate yourself at "Follow through, follow up?" Do you turn out the light when walking out of the room? Do you throw away your gum wrapper? Do you put your shoes and bags in the right spot when you get home? Depending on your personality, it may be easy for you to follow up because you enjoy organization. If you are like a lot of students, you may leave a disaster path in your wake, and someone can easily tell whether you brushed your teeth, what flavor of pop-tart you ate for breakfast, what chips you chose for lunch and what you did all day….because everything is left everywhere! Great leaders learn to follow through with tasks and follow up by putting away what they use. Say it out loud, "Follow through, follow up." "Follow through, follow up." Now, do that!

WHAT YOU LEARNED ○ DAY 5

Did you learn more about God's Love or God's Plan? Maybe you learned more about His Character or Truth. Place a checkmark in the box next to what you feel you learned about God. Then take a minute to write what you learned.

○ **GOD'S LOVE**

○ **GOD'S CHARACTER**

○ **GOD'S TRUTH**

○ **GOD'S PLAN**

Finish these final steps for today's journal. Checkmark each completed task.

● **HOW DO YOU PLAN TO MAKE THIS A PART OF YOUR EVERY DAY LIFE?**
[Write your answer in the appropriate **MY PLAN** Box in the back of this journal]

● **WHAT IS ONE POTENTIAL AREA OF WEAKNESS YOU WILL ASK THE HOLY SPIRIT TO HELP YOU MAKE STRONGER?**

[Stop now and ask the Holy Spirit for help in this area]

● **ENCOURAGE A FRIEND**
[Share empowering thoughts, ideas, words, and scriptures with your friends. Know what's going on in your friends lives. Make those things a matter of prayer. Find and share scriptures to encourage them.]

THE NAME OF THE FRIEND YOU ENCOURAGED:

THIS IS WHAT I DID: [circle all that you did]

called them   texted them   emailed them   talked to them   wrote a lette

50

MY PERSONAL NOTES

Read the principle and the scriptures below. These are the ideas you want to have strong in your heart. Take your time and think about what you are reading. When you have finished this page, place a checkmark next to DAY 1.

PRINCIPLE

DON'T SKIMP!

In the summer, don't you love going to your favorite ice cream stand and ordering a cone? Have you ever received one much larger than normal because the person was generous with the serving? So great! But, have you ever gotten a skimpy one because the person was in a hurry, or maybe wasn't great at making cones? That's super disappointing! As a good leader, skimping on a job, or with your attitude is just stinky for the person on the receiving end. Make sure you're serving with generosity and excellence! No one likes to be skimped on!!

SCRIPTURES
Growing in your knowledge of the Word.

☐ Whoever can be trusted with very little can also be trusted with much, and whoever is dishonest with very little will also be dishonest with much. Luke 16:10 NIV

☐ Whatever you do, work at it with all your heart, as working for the Lord, not for human masters. Colossians 3:23 NIV

☐ Work hard and become a leader; be lazy and become a slave. Proverbs 12:24 NLT

Place a check-mark next to the scripture you plan to memorize this week. Once you have recited it to a parent or leader, write the scripture in the appropriate box on your Memorized Word page.

For the next three days, you will read the lesson below. For each day you will mark the part of the lesson that stands out to you on that day. Each day requires you to use a different method. When you have completed marking the lesson for that day, checkmark the circle.

◯DAY 2 | <u>Underline</u>   ◯DAY 3 | (Circle)   ◯DAY 4 | [Bracket]

I RUN THROUGH THE FINISH LINE!

To win a sprint race, you must run through the finish line! If you only run to the line, you slow down before you get there! When you run through it, your body crosses the line at full speed! Likewise, when you are given a job, you must run through the finish line! But how? Pay attention. Go the extra mile. Don't simply do the minimum. Have you had the privilege of trash duty? What? A privilege?! Yes! Trash duty can teach you so much! When you empty the kitchen trash, just taking the bag out is the minimum. Running through the finish line would be removing the trash bag from the can. Then, paying attention to pick up miscellaneous pieces that are on the floor around the trash can, and throwing them away too. After that, ensuring that the trash can is returned to its exact place, putting another trash liner in it, and even turning out the light when you are done! See the difference? Running through the finish line ensures everything is complete and excellent! So next time you have chores to do, run through the finish line not just to it!

Did you learn more about God's Love or God's Plan? Maybe you learned more about His Character or Truth. Place a checkmark in the box next to what you feel you learned about God. Then take a minute to write what you learned.

○ **GOD'S LOVE**

○ **GOD'S CHARACTER**

○ **GOD'S TRUTH**

○ **GOD'S PLAN**

Finish these final steps for today's journal. Checkmark each completed task.

● **HOW DO YOU PLAN TO MAKE THIS A PART OF YOUR EVERY DAY LIFE?**
[Write your answer in the appropriate **MY PLAN** Box in the back of this journal]

● **WHAT IS ONE POTENTIAL AREA OF WEAKNESS YOU WILL ASK THE HOLY SPIRIT TO HELP YOU MAKE STRONGER?**

[Stop now and ask the Holy Spirit for help in this area]

● **ENCOURAGE A FRIEND**
[Share empowering thoughts, ideas, words, and scriptures with your friends. Know what's going on in your friends lives. Make those things a matter of prayer. Find and share scriptures to encourage them.]

THE NAME OF THE FRIEND YOU ENCOURAGED:

THIS IS WHAT I DID: [circle all that you did]

called them   texted them   emailed them   talked to them   wrote a lette

54

MY PERSONAL NOTES

Read the principle and the scriptures below. These are the ideas you want to have strong in your heart. Take your time and think about what you are reading. When you have finished this page, place a checkmark next to DAY 1.

PRINCIPLE

HONOR UP, HONOR DOWN, HONOR ALL AROUND

We honor others when we recognize that they are important and valuable, treating everyone with respect. We honor up – God, our parents, our teachers, our mentors, those who have authority in our lives. We honor down – students who may be following us and our younger siblings. We honor all around – those who are our peers and friends. We treat everyone we encounter as important because they are! They are divinely created by God and have great value. We honor up, down, and all around. We treat everyone with great respect!

SCRIPTURES

Growing in your knowledge of the Word.

- [ ] Pride leads to destruction, and arrogance to downfall. Proverbs 16:18 GNT

- [ ] If you honor your father and mother, "things will go well for you, and you will have a long life on the earth." Ephesians 6:3 NLT

- [ ] Therefore He says: "God resists the proud, But gives grace to the humble." James 4:6 NKJV

Place a check-mark next to the scripture you plan to memorize this week. Once you have recited it to a parent or leader, write the scripture in the appropriate box on your Memorized Word page.

For the next three days, you will read the lesson below. For each day you will mark the part of the lesson that stands out to you on that day. Each day requires you to use a different method. When you have completed marking the lesson for that day, checkmark the circle.

◯DAY 2 | <u>Underline</u>   ◯DAY 3 | Circle   ◯DAY 4 | [Bracket]

PRIDE COMES BEFORE A FALL

If we think we are better than others, we are being influenced by pride. When we think our parents or mentors our weird, old-fashioned, or don't know as much as we do about something, we are being influenced by pride. When we belittle our siblings or friends, making fun of them or tearing them down so we feel better about ourselves, we are being influenced by pride. Pride is ugly and arrogant, always trying to get us to believe we are better than others. But pride is not our friend. The Bible says "pride leads to destruction, and arrogance to downfall." That is why it is so important to walk in humility and honor. Humility and honor keep us in check. They cause us to realize that we are not more valuable than our parents or teachers or siblings or peers. We are not more valuable than people of a different race or nationality or social class. God has made every person with incredible value; when we treat others with humility and respect, we actually show great honor to God. Pride comes before a fall but humility brings God's grace and favor.

www.KUEST.org

WHAT YOU LEARNED ⃝ DAY 5

Did you learn more about God's Love or God's Plan? Maybe you learned more about His Character or Truth. Place a checkmark in the box next to what you feel you learned about God. Then take a minute to write what you learned.

⃝ **GOD'S LOVE**

⃝ **GOD'S CHARACTER**

⃝ **GOD'S TRUTH**

⃝ **GOD'S PLAN**

Finish these final steps for today's journal. Checkmark each completed task.

⃝ **HOW DO YOU PLAN TO MAKE THIS A PART OF YOUR EVERY DAY LIFE?**
[Write your answer in the appropriate **MY PLAN** Box in the back of this journal]

⃝ **WHAT IS ONE POTENTIAL AREA OF WEAKNESS YOU WILL ASK THE HOLY SPIRIT TO HELP YOU MAKE STRONGER?**

[Stop now and ask the Holy Spirit for help in this area]

⃝ **ENCOURAGE A FRIEND**
[Share empowering thoughts, ideas, words, and scriptures with your friends. Know what's going on in your friends lives. Make those things a matter of prayer. Find and share scriptures to encourage them.]

THE NAME OF THE FRIEND YOU ENCOURAGED:

THIS IS WHAT I DID: [circle all that you did]

called them   texted them   emailed them   talked to them   wrote a lette

58

MY PERSONAL NOTES

WEEK #15
◯ DAY 1

Read the principle and the scriptures below. These are the ideas you want to have strong in your heart. Take your time and think about what you are reading. When you have finished this page, place a checkmark next to DAY 1.

PRINCIPLE

I WILL LOVE MY LIFE AND SEE GOOD DAYS

Do you want to love your life and enjoy good days? The Bible gives you the key: control your mouth! By keeping your tongue from speaking hurtful, evil words and by choosing to be honest, did you know that you can actually set the course for your life? How often are your words positive about you? About others? About what you have and what you get to do? Are you honest? These things make a difference in how well you actually enjoy your life! So, take your talking pattern from God's Word and love your life!

SCRIPTURES
Growing in your knowledge of the Word.

☐ The tongue can bring death or life; those who love to talk will reap the consequences. Proverbs 18:21 NLT

☐ Can both fresh water and saltwater flow from the same spring? James 3:11 NIV

☐ As the scripture says, "If you want to enjoy life and wish to see good times, you must keep from speaking evil and stop telling lies. 1 Peter 3:10 GNT

Place a check-mark next to the scripture you plan to memorize this week. Once you have recited it to a parent or leader, write the scripture in the appropriate box on your Memorized Word page.

60

◯ DAYS 2-4

STRONGER HEART

For the next three days, you will read the lesson below. For each day you will mark the part of the lesson that stands out to you on that day. Each day requires you to use a different method. When you have completed marking the lesson for that day, checkmark the circle.

◯ DAY 2 | <u>Underline</u>   ◯ DAY 3 | (Circle)   ◯ DAY 4 | [Bracket]

I GET TO CHOOSE LIFE OR DEATH

When you were a kid, did you ever do the science experiment of planting a small seed in a paper cup? If you planted a flower seed, before long you enjoyed a pretty, little flower. If you planted a bean seed, shortly after a little bean plant popped up. We know that whatever plant we get is because of the seed we choose. Did you know that is exactly how your words work? The Bible teaches us that our words are seeds. Every time that we speak words, some type of seeds are flying out of our mouth, planting what we will experience in the future. What are you saying about yourself, your grades, how people treat you, what your future looks like? Whatever you are saying is exactly what you will get! You have the power to speak good, positive things that will bring success to your life, and you also have the power to speak negative, evil things that will bring hurt and failure into your life. Choose to speak good things and you will enjoy life and see good days!

61

WHAT YOU LEARNED ○ DAY 5

Did you learn more about God's Love or God's Plan? Maybe you learned more about His Character or Truth. Place a checkmark in the box next to what you feel you learned about God. Then take a minute to write what you learned.

○ **GOD'S LOVE**

○ **GOD'S CHARACTER**

○ **GOD'S TRUTH**

○ **GOD'S PLAN**

Finish these final steps for today's journal. Checkmark each completed task.

● **HOW DO YOU PLAN TO MAKE THIS A PART OF YOUR EVERY DAY LIFE?**
[Write your answer in the appropriate **MY PLAN** Box in the back of this journal]

● **WHAT IS ONE POTENTIAL AREA OF WEAKNESS YOU WILL ASK THE HOLY SPIRIT TO HELP YOU MAKE STRONGER?**

[Stop now and ask the Holy Spirit for help in this area]

● **ENCOURAGE A FRIEND**
[Share empowering thoughts, ideas, words, and scriptures with your friends. Know what's going on in your friends lives. Make those things a matter of prayer. Find and share scriptures to encourage them.]

THE NAME OF THE FRIEND YOU ENCOURAGED:

THIS IS WHAT I DID: [circle all that you did]

called them   texted them   emailed them   talked to them   wrote a letter

62

MY PERSONAL NOTES

Read the principle and the scriptures below. These are the ideas you want to have strong in your heart. Take your time and think about what you are reading. When you have finished this page, place a checkmark next to DAY 1.

PRINCIPLE

I USE MY CREATIVE SUPER POWERS

You may not realize it, but there is a Super Power on the inside of you. God placed it in every human, but very few ever discover and use it! What is this Super Power, you ask? It is the ability to create your future, to change a circumstance that you don't like, and to build a successful life – with your words! God has this Super Power and He has put it in you! You are made in His image – and your words have power!

SCRIPTURES
Growing in your knowledge of the Word.

☐ …in the presence of the God in whom he believed, who gives life to the dead and calls into existence the things that do not exist. Romans 4:17 ESV

☐ So God created human beings in his own image. In the image of God he created them; male and female he created them. Genesis 1:27 NLT

☐ For assuredly, I say to you, whoever says to this mountain, "Be removed and be cast into the sea," and does not doubt in his heart, but believes that those things he says will be done, he will have whatever he says. Mark 11:23 NKJV

Place a check-mark next to the scripture you plan to memorize this week. Once you have recited it to a parent or leader, write the scripture in the appropriate box on your Memorized Word page.

64

For the next three days, you will read the lesson below. For each day you will mark the part of the lesson that stands out to you on that day. Each day requires you to use a different method. When you have completed marking the lesson for that day, checkmark the circle.

○DAY 2 | <u>Underline</u>　○DAY 3 | Ⓒircle　○DAY 4 | [Bracket]

I CALL IT!

Is there a situation about your relationships, school, fear about your future, that has you frustrated or down? You can begin to turn it around with your words! In the beginning, God looked at the earth that was dark, without life or anything fun. He didn't want it that way. So, what did He do? He spoke WORDS to change it! He said, "Let there be light…." And things started to change! The Bible describes God as the One "who gives life to the dead and calls into existence the things that do not exist."

God made you in His image and put this same ability in you! Just like an umpire calls the play, God gave you authority to call the plays in your life. You have the ability to call situations the way you want them to be! You can call your science grade "better and better". You can call yourself disciplined and happy with great friends. You can call your mind peaceful and free from fear. How are you going to call it? Call it good! Call it fun! Call it successful! And that's how it is going to be!

www.KUEST.org

Did you learn more about God's Love or God's Plan? Maybe you learned more about His Character or Truth. Place a checkmark in the box next to what you feel you learned about God. Then take a minute to write what you learned.

○ **GOD'S LOVE**

○ **GOD'S CHARACTER**

○ **GOD'S TRUTH**

○ **GOD'S PLAN**

Finish these final steps for today's journal. Checkmark each completed task.

● **HOW DO YOU PLAN TO MAKE THIS A PART OF YOUR EVERY DAY LIFE?**

[Write your answer in the appropriate **MY PLAN** Box in the back of this journal]

● **WHAT IS ONE POTENTIAL AREA OF WEAKNESS YOU WILL ASK THE HOLY SPIRIT TO HELP YOU MAKE STRONGER?**

[Stop now and ask the Holy Spirit for help in this area]

● **ENCOURAGE A FRIEND**

[Share empowering thoughts, ideas, words, and scriptures with your friends. Know what's going on in your friends lives. Make those things a matter of prayer. Find and share scriptures to encourage them.]

THE NAME OF THE FRIEND YOU ENCOURAGED:

THIS IS WHAT I DID: [circle all that you did]

called them   texted them   emailed them   talked to them   wrote a letter

66

MY PERSONAL NOTES

Read the principle and the scriptures below. These are the ideas you want to have strong in your heart. Take your time and think about what you are reading. When you have finished this page, place a checkmark next to DAY 1.

PRINCIPLE

I POSITION MYSELF TO LEARN

Wouldn't it be great if we just knew everything? Instead of having to spend so many hours in school learning, we would already know every subject! Instead of having to learn something from a consequence, we would already know the right way to do things! The truth is that as long as you are breathing, you will have more to learn. The more you position yourself to learn, the better your life will be. There is always more to know, and when you position yourself to learn, you will always grow and get better.

SCRIPTURES
Growing in your knowledge of the Word.

☐ The fear of the Lord is the beginning of knowledge; fools despise wisdom and instruction. Proverbs 1:7 ESV

☐ Wise people treasure knowledge, but the babbling of a fool invites disaster. Proverbs 10:14 NLT

☐ Don't think you are better than you really are. Be honest in your evaluation of yourselves, measuring yourselves by the faith God has given us. Romans 12:3 NLT

Place a check-mark next to the scripture you plan to memorize this week. Once you have recited it to a parent or leader, write the scripture in the appropriate box on your Memorized Word page.

68

○ DAYS 2-4

STRONGER HEART

For the next three days, you will read the lesson below. For each day you will mark the part of the lesson that stands out to you on that day. Each day requires you to use a different method. When you have completed marking the lesson for that day, checkmark the circle.

○ DAY 2 | <u>Underline</u>   ○ DAY 3 | (Circle)   ○ DAY 4 | [Bracket]

I'M NO FOOL!

What comes to mind when you hear the words "dummy", "idiot", "ignoramous", "dufus"? Do these describe someone who applies themselves to be their best, takes learning seriously, and desires to understand new things and grow? Of course not! Would you want these words to describe you? No way! These words portray what Scripture calls a "fool" - a stupid person who lacks judgment or sense. Fools are students who choose to not listen to parents, mentors and those in authority. Fools are those who think they know everything. Instead of valuing knowledge and positioning themselves to learn, they just talk all the time about what they think. Do you honor and appreciate parents, mentors and peers who are skillful in a certain area? Do you value learning so you can continuously improve? As you position yourself in humility and choose to treasure knowledge, you put yourself in the category of the wise! Fools hate knowledge and hate learning. So remember, on those days when learning seems miserable, choose to embrace learning! It will keep you from being a fool.

www.KUEST.org

WHAT YOU LEARNED ◯ DAY 5

Did you learn more about God's Love or God's Plan? Maybe you learned more about His Character or Truth. Place a checkmark in the box next to what you feel you learned about God. Then take a minute to write what you learned.

◯ **GOD'S LOVE**

◯ **GOD'S CHARACTER**

◯ **GOD'S TRUTH**

◯ **GOD'S PLAN**

Finish these final steps for today's journal. Checkmark each completed task.

⬤ **HOW DO YOU PLAN TO MAKE THIS A PART OF YOUR EVERY DAY LIFE?**
[Write your answer in the appropriate **MY PLAN** Box in the back of this journal]

⬤ **WHAT IS ONE POTENTIAL AREA OF WEAKNESS YOU WILL ASK THE HOLY SPIRIT TO HELP YOU MAKE STRONGER?**

[Stop now and ask the Holy Spirit for help in this area]

⬤ **ENCOURAGE A FRIEND**
[Share empowering thoughts, ideas, words, and scriptures with your friends. Know what's going on in your friends lives. Make those things a matter of prayer. Find and share scriptures to encourage them.]

THE NAME OF THE FRIEND YOU ENCOURAGED:

THIS IS WHAT I DID: [circle all that you did]

called them   texted them   emailed them   talked to them   wrote a letter

70

MY PERSONAL
NOTES

Read the principle and the scriptures below. These are the ideas you want to have strong in your heart. Take your time and think about what you are reading. When you have finished this page, place a checkmark next to DAY 1.

PRINCIPLE

MAKE LIFE A PARTY!

After God created the earth, He looked and saw that everything was good – except for one thing. He recognized that Adam was alone and that he needed someone to love and live life with him. He needed a friend to encourage and celebrate him. These are hugely important! When others compliment us and express how great we are, it literally puts courage on the inside of us. They can cause us to feel like we can do anything! Your words bring that kind of life and courage! So throw a party with your words – and encourage others!

SCRIPTURES

Growing in your knowledge of the Word.

☐ When others are happy, be happy with them, and when they are sad, be sad. Romans 12:15 CEV

☐ Worry weighs a person down; an encouraging word cheers a person up. Proverbs 12:25 NLT

☐ Don't use foul or abusive language. Let everything you say be good and helpful, so that your words will be an encouragement to those who hear them. Ephesians 4:29 NLT

Place a check-mark next to the scripture you plan to memorize this week. Once you have recited it to a parent or leader, write the scripture in the appropriate box on your Memorized Word page.

For the next three days, you will read the lesson below. For each day you will mark the part of the lesson that stands out to you on that day. Each day requires you to use a different method. When you have completed marking the lesson for that day, checkmark the circle.

⭕ **DAY 2 | <u>Underline</u>**   ⭕ **DAY 3 | Ⓒircle**   ⭕ **DAY 4 | [Bracket]**

THROW CONFETTI!

What an amazing feeling it is to accomplish something great and be celebrated! And isn't it so fun when friends and family celebrate with you? It makes you feel so valuable and important! We all love that, but how well do you celebrate others? Sometimes we can feel like we want to withhold encouragement, and not cheer our friends on. Not celebrating others is huge sign of pride. However, when you carry a party inside you and pour excitement and celebration on your family and friends, you don't ever have to worry about missing out on being celebrated! God promises that what you sow, you reap. If you throw a party for your friends, God makes sure someone throws a party for you. If you live a life celebrating and encouraging others, that is what will come back to you! But if you withhold your cheer....you'll reap that from others. Leaders don't ever withhold celebration. As a great leader, we throw confetti! We celebrate others! Make others feel like the greatest person in the world! You won't miss out because God sees it! And He will cue the confetti for you!

WHAT YOU LEARNED ◯DAY 5

Did you learn more about God's Love or God's Plan? Maybe you learned more about His Character or Truth. Place a checkmark in the box next to what you feel you learned about God. Then take a minute to write what you learned.

◯ **GOD'S LOVE**

◯ **GOD'S CHARACTER**

◯ **GOD'S TRUTH**

◯ **GOD'S PLAN**

Finish these final steps for today's journal. Checkmark each completed task.

◯ **HOW DO YOU PLAN TO MAKE THIS A PART OF YOUR EVERY DAY LIFE?**
[Write your answer in the appropriate **MY PLAN** Box in the back of this journal]

◯ **WHAT IS ONE POTENTIAL AREA OF WEAKNESS YOU WILL ASK THE HOLY SPIRIT TO HELP YOU MAKE STRONGER?**

[Stop now and ask the Holy Spirit for help in this area]

● **ENCOURAGE A FRIEND**
[Share empowering thoughts, ideas, words, and scriptures with your friends. Know what's going on in your friends lives. Make those things a matter of prayer. Find and share scriptures to encourage them.]

THE NAME OF THE FRIEND YOU ENCOURAGED:

THIS IS WHAT I DID: [circle all that you did]

called them   texted them   emailed them   talked to them   wrote a letter

MY PERSONAL NOTES

Read the principle and the scriptures below. These are the ideas you want to have strong in your heart. Take your time and think about what you are reading. When you have finished this page, place a checkmark next to DAY 1.

PRINCIPLE

I'VE GOT THIS!

Procrastination. It's a big word, but many do it every day by choosing to put off a chore or assignment until later because they just don't feel like doing it. Do you ever procrastinate? Good leaders knock out their chores and assignments instead of putting things off. Do you know that the longer you procrastinate, the more you begin to dread? You can waste hours and days dreading what you have to do! Don't let dread and procrastination eat up all your time. Tell yourself, "I've got this!" Tackle what needs done, then be free the rest of your day!

SCRIPTURES
Growing in your knowledge of the Word.

☐ But be sure that everything is done properly and in order.
1 Corinthians 14:40 NLT

☐ No discipline seems pleasant at the time, but painful. Later on, however, it produces a harvest of righteousness and peace for those who have been trained by it. Hebrews 12:11 NIV

☐ A lazy person is as bad as someone who destroys things.
Proverbs 18:9 NLT

Place a check-mark next to the scripture you plan to memorize this week. Once you have recited it to a parent or leader, write the scripture in the appropriate box on your Memorized Word page.

For the next three days, you will read the lesson below. For each day you will mark the part of the lesson that stands out to you on that day. Each day requires you to use a different method. When you have completed marking the lesson for that day, checkmark the circle.

○ **DAY 2 | Underline**   ○ **DAY 3 | Circle**   ○ **DAY 4 | [Bracket]**

ONE BITE AT A TIME

Have you ever heard the question, "How do you eat an elephant?" The answer: "One bite at a time!" What in the world does this mean? It's the secret to great accomplishments, to things that may seem too big or overwhelming. If you allow them, procrastination and dread can keep you from growing, getting better and accomplishing great things! But if you tackle things "one bite at a time" you will constantly make progress, no matter how large the task or how impossible something may seem! To improve yourself in any area, to increase your skills, to create something new, or to build something great, you will be required every day to knock out tasks. Practice and keep practicing. Exercise and don't quit. Write, one word at a time. Read how-to's. Watch Tutorials. Try new things. Track your progress. To complete a project, whether a school assignment like a major report, or something you desire to do on your own, like creating a song, getting physically fit, or improving your tennis serve, go after a little bite of it every day. If you don't quit, you will someday see that you have conquered the entire elephant!

WHAT YOU LEARNED ○DAY 5

Did you learn more about God's Love or God's Plan? Maybe you learned more about His Character or Truth. Place a checkmark in the box next to what you feel you learned about God. Then take a minute to write what you learned.

○ **GOD'S LOVE**

○ **GOD'S CHARACTER**

○ **GOD'S TRUTH**

○ **GOD'S PLAN**

Finish these final steps for today's journal. Checkmark each completed task.

● **HOW DO YOU PLAN TO MAKE THIS A PART OF YOUR EVERY DAY LIFE?**
[Write your answer in the appropriate **MY PLAN** Box in the back of this journal]

● **WHAT IS ONE POTENTIAL AREA OF WEAKNESS YOU WILL ASK THE HOLY SPIRIT TO HELP YOU MAKE STRONGER?**

[Stop now and ask the Holy Spirit for help in this area]

● **ENCOURAGE A FRIEND**
[Share empowering thoughts, ideas, words, and scriptures with your friends. Know what's going on in your friends lives. Make those things a matter of prayer. Find and share scriptures to encourage them.]

THE NAME OF THE FRIEND YOU ENCOURAGED:

THIS IS WHAT I DID: [circle all that you did]

called them   texted them   emailed them   talked to them   wrote a letter

78

MY PERSONAL NOTES

Read the principle and the scriptures below. These are the ideas you want to have strong in your heart. Take your time and think about what you are reading. When you have finished this page, place a checkmark next to DAY 1.

PRINCIPLE
NO-CRASH ZONE

Have you ever seen a major NASCAR race? It's amazing how fast drivers fly around the track! And, when a car crashes, it's breath-taking to look through the smoke to see who else gets caught in the crash and if the drivers are OK! As great leaders, we should make sure we are living a "no crash zone" kind of life, one that ensures our safety and the safety of anyone following us. Bible wisdom protects us and keeps us safe. As a great leader, when we follow Bible wisdom, we safely put ourselves in the "no crash zone!"

SCRIPTURES
Growing in your knowledge of the Word.

☐ Do not abandon wisdom, and she will protect you; love her, and she will keep you safe. Proverbs 4:6 GNT

☐ Therefore everyone who hears these words of mine and puts them into practice is like a wise man who built his house on the rock. Matthew 7:24 NIV

☐ But everyone who hears these words of mine and does not put them into practice is like a foolish man who built his house on sand. The rain came down, the streams rose, and the winds blew and beat against that house, and it fell with a great crash." Matthew 7:26-27 NIV

Place a check-mark next to the scripture you plan to memorize this week. Once you have recited it to a parent or leader, write the scripture in the appropriate box on your Memorized Word page.

⭕ DAYS 2-4

STRONGER HEART

For the next three days, you will read the lesson below. For each day you will mark the part of the lesson that stands out to you on that day. Each day requires you to use a different method. When you have completed marking the lesson for that day, checkmark the circle.

⭕ DAY 2 | <u>Underline</u>   ⭕ DAY 3 | (Circle)   ⭕ DAY 4 | [Bracket]

AVOID DISASTER, BUILD YOUR LIFE WISELY

Like adventure? You would love the Willis Tower Ledge in Chicago. It's the tallest building in the Western Hemisphere that takes you 1,353 feet in the air. On the 103rd floor, you can walk out into a glass box and see an exhilarating view of downtown Chicago and up to 50 miles and 4 states! Would go up into this skyscraper if it wasn't securely built? If the foundation was just a couple of bricks, would you feel secure 103 feet into the sky? Obviously, the foundation of this building required massive amounts of concrete and steel to ensure that it would stay solid, especially during strong winds and storms. Just like the great effort and construction of this foundation, The Bible tells us to put great effort into the foundation we choose to build our life on. The ONLY secure foundation is Jesus. We build our life on Him, His Love, and the Truth we read in The Word. If we choose to build our life on other opinions, we will experience great crashes in our life. When you believe God's Word and make all your decisions based on Bible Truth, you are guaranteed a secure, awesome life.

WHAT YOU LEARNED ○ DAY 5

Did you learn more about God's Love or God's Plan? Maybe you learned more about His Character or Truth. Place a checkmark in the box next to what you feel you learned about God. Then take a minute to write what you learned.

○ **GOD'S LOVE**

○ **GOD'S CHARACTER**

○ **GOD'S TRUTH**

○ **GOD'S PLAN**

Finish these final steps for today's journal. Checkmark each completed task.

● **HOW DO YOU PLAN TO MAKE THIS A PART OF YOUR EVERY DAY LIFE?**
[Write your answer in the appropriate **MY PLAN** Box in the back of this journal]

● **WHAT IS ONE POTENTIAL AREA OF WEAKNESS YOU WILL ASK THE HOLY SPIRIT TO HELP YOU MAKE STRONGER?**

[Stop now and ask the Holy Spirit for help in this area]

● **ENCOURAGE A FRIEND**
[Share empowering thoughts, ideas, words, and scriptures with your friends. Know what's going on in your friends lives. Make those things a matter of prayer. Find and share scriptures to encourage them.]

THE NAME OF THE FRIEND YOU ENCOURAGED:

THIS IS WHAT I DID: [circle all that you did]

called them   texted them   emailed them   talked to them   wrote a letter

82

MY PERSONAL NOTES

Read the principle and the scriptures below. These are the ideas you want to have strong in your heart. Take your time and think about what you are reading. When you have finished this page, place a checkmark next to DAY 1.

PRINCIPLE

STAY ON GOD'S SIDE

Have you ever felt frustrated or disappointed at God? When something goes wrong, it's not God's fault! And, putting yourself against God is the wrong place to be! He is Love. He is only Good. He never hurts or disappoints us. When there are things we don't understand, don't blame God! Stay on His Side! He is for you and desires to help you. When you walk through something hurtful, stay on God's Side! Run to Him for comfort, peace and help. He promises to make a way for you and work and everything out for your good!

SCRIPTURES
Growing in your knowledge of the Word.

☐ For the eyes of the Lord run to and fro throughout the whole earth, to show Himself strong on behalf of *those* whose heart *is* loyal to Him. 2 Chronicles 16:9 NKJV

☐ If God is for us, who can be against us? Romans 8:31 NIV

☐ And we know that God causes everything to work together for the good of those who love God and are called according to his purpose for them. Romans 8:28 NLT

Place a check-mark next to the scripture you plan to memorize this week. Once you have recited it to a parent or leader, write the scripture in the appropriate box on your Memorized Word page.

84

STRONGER HEART

For the next three days, you will read the lesson below. For each day you will mark the part of the lesson that stands out to you on that day. Each day requires you to use a different method. When you have completed marking the lesson for that day, checkmark the circle.

○DAY 2 | <u>Underline</u>   ○DAY 3 | Circle   ○DAY 4 | [Bracket]

CHOOSE GOD'S SIDE

Have you ever had two friends disagree? And then they escaladed from a small grudge into a full-blown fight? It's easy to feel caught in the middle, like you have to choose sides. But you don't have to feel pressured to take a side! You can choose God's side – by remaining a friend to both of them. Culture will always try to force us to choose a side. Whether it's sports teams or social current events, political debates or even sometimes in relationships, you can feel pressured to choose a side. But you don't ever have to cave to the pressure. There is only one side to which you should be loyal, and that is God's Side! Choosing God's side is simply aligning with what God's Word says about every situation. Are your friends talking negatively about each other? God's side is for you to walk in love, refusing to gossip or argue. Be an example to others and help them see that God's side is the higher road. It's above pressure. It keeps you free and in peace. Choose God's Side!

WHAT YOU LEARNED ◯DAY 5

Did you learn more about God's Love or God's Plan? Maybe you learned more about His Character or Truth. Place a checkmark in the box next to what you feel you learned about God. Then take a minute to write what you learned.

◯ **GOD'S LOVE**

◯ **GOD'S CHARACTER**

◯ **GOD'S TRUTH**

◯ **GOD'S PLAN**

Finish these final steps for today's journal. Checkmark each completed task.

● **HOW DO YOU PLAN TO MAKE THIS A PART OF YOUR EVERY DAY LIFE?**
[Write your answer in the appropriate **MY PLAN** Box in the back of this journal]

● **WHAT IS ONE POTENTIAL AREA OF WEAKNESS YOU WILL ASK THE HOLY SPIRIT TO HELP YOU MAKE STRONGER?**

[Stop now and ask the Holy Spirit for help in this area]

● **ENCOURAGE A FRIEND**
[Share empowering thoughts, ideas, words, and scriptures with your friends. Know what's going on in your friends lives. Make those things a matter of prayer. Find and share scriptures to encourage them.]

THE NAME OF THE FRIEND YOU ENCOURAGED:

THIS IS WHAT I DID: [circle all that you did]

called them   texted them   emailed them   talked to them   wrote a letter

86

MY PERSONAL
NOTES

Read the principle and the scriptures below. These are the ideas you want to have strong in your heart. Take your time and think about what you are reading. When you have finished this page, place a checkmark next to DAY 1.

PRINCIPLE

IF IT'S GOING TO BE ITS UP TO ME

Living in God's amazing plan for your life is your choice! God has already written an incredible story for you and made a way to live a life beyond your wildest dreams! Did you know it's your choice to cooperate with God to enjoy success and happiness? God's Plan is His Best for you, but He has given you a free will. You choose to walk in God's Plan or do your own thing by choosing to cooperate or resist Him. His plan for you is incredible! So choose His Plan!

SCRIPTURES
Growing in your knowledge of the Word.

☐ God can do anything, you know—far more than you could ever imagine or guess or request in your wildest dreams! He does it not by pushing us around but by working within us, his Spirit deeply and gently within us. Ephesians 3:20-21 MSG

☐ The thief's purpose is to steal and kill and destroy. My purpose is to give them a rich and satisfying life. John 10:10 NLT

☐ You saw me before I was born. Every day of my life was recorded in your book. Every moment was laid out before a single day had passed. Psalm 139:16 NLT

Place a check-mark next to the scripture you plan to memorize this week. Once you have recited it to a parent or leader, write the scripture in the appropriate box on your Memorized Word page.

88

For the next three days, you will read the lesson below. For each day you will mark the part of the lesson that stands out to you on that day. Each day requires you to use a different method. When you have completed marking the lesson for that day, checkmark the circle.

○ DAY 2 | <u>Underline</u>   ○ DAY 3 | Ⓒircle   ○ DAY 4 | [Bracket]

I HOLD MYSELF ACCOUNTABLE

Just think, God really does have a book with every day of His Plan for your life mapped out. He sent Jesus to give you an incredible life! God also sent the Holy Spirit to live in you, giving you wisdom and power to tap into His Master Plan! God has set you up! Now think of everything your parents have given! Think of all that your parents, teachers, coaches, and mentors have done to help educate and train, sharpen your talents and gifts, give you practical life skills, love, confidence and encouragement, so that you can have success. Even with all that God and your parents have done, do you realize that if you do not engage your heart and soul to know God and to cooperate with Him, if you choose not to apply yourself for success, not even God or your parents can make your life great? You must hold yourself accountable to know God and seek His Plan for your life. You must hold yourself accountable to discipline and faithfulness in your studies and other pursuits. Use your strength to hold yourself accountable and live an amazing life full of fun and success!

www.KUEST.org

WHAT YOU LEARNED ○DAY 5

Did you learn more about God's Love or God's Plan? Maybe you learned more about His Character or Truth. Place a checkmark in the box next to what you feel you learned about God. Then take a minute to write what you learned.

○ **GOD'S LOVE**

○ **GOD'S CHARACTER**

○ **GOD'S TRUTH**

○ **GOD'S PLAN**

Finish these final steps for today's journal. Checkmark each completed task.

● **HOW DO YOU PLAN TO MAKE THIS A PART OF YOUR EVERY DAY LIFE?**
[Write your answer in the appropriate **MY PLAN** Box in the back of this journal]

● **WHAT IS ONE POTENTIAL AREA OF WEAKNESS YOU WILL ASK THE HOLY SPIRIT TO HELP YOU MAKE STRONGER?**

[Stop now and ask the Holy Spirit for help in this area]

● **ENCOURAGE A FRIEND**
[Share empowering thoughts, ideas, words, and scriptures with your friends. Know what's going on in your friends lives. Make those things a matter of prayer. Find and share scriptures to encourage them.]

THE NAME OF THE FRIEND YOU ENCOURAGED:

THIS IS WHAT I DID: [circle all that you did]

called them   texted them   emailed them   talked to them   wrote a letter

90

MY PERSONAL NOTES

Read the principle and the scriptures below. These are the ideas you want to have strong in your heart. Take your time and think about what you are reading. When you have finished this page, place a checkmark next to DAY 1.

PRINCIPLE

THE SECRET SAUCE

Have you ever valued someone successful? A singer, a golfer, a doctor, a good Mom, a valedictorian, an Olympian? It doesn't matter in what area they are accomplished, there is a secret sauce behind their success. Interestingly, the secret sauce usually isn't talent. The secret sauce is their daily routine – how they choose to spend their time. This includes good things they say, "yes" to every day, and distractions they say, "no" to. How would you create your secret sauce for success? What is your daily routine? Determine how you will spend time each day developing the best you!

SCRIPTURES
Growing in your knowledge of the Word.

☐ Take a lesson from the ants, you lazybones. Learn from their ways and become wise! Proverbs 6:6 NLT

☐ Lazy people are soon poor; hard workers get rich. Proverbs 10:4 NLT

☐ So let's not get tired of doing what is good. At just the right time we will reap a harvest of blessing if we don't give up. Galatians 6:9 NIV

Place a check-mark next to the scripture you plan to memorize this week. Once you have recited it to a parent or leader, write the scripture in the appropriate box on your Memorized Word page.

92

STRONGER
HEART

For the next three days, you will read the lesson below. For each day you will mark the part of the lesson that stands out to you on that day. Each day requires you to use a different method. When you have completed marking the lesson for that day, checkmark the circle.

○ DAY 2 | <u>Underline</u>   ○ DAY 3 | Circle   ○ DAY 4 | [Bracket]

THE SECRET TO MY SUCCESS

Life Coach, John Maxwell, said, "The secret of your success is found in your daily routine." In other words, what you do every day leads you somewhere. If your daily routine is full of discipline and consistency, where you engage in growing yourself, exercising spiritually, mentally and physically, and sharpening your skills, those daily actions will lead you to success. If you go through your days being lazy and distracted, where you don't put much effort into growing or increasing your skills and knowledge, and you allow your emotions to dictate your day, those daily actions will lead you away from success. Successful people have goals and they work toward them. They have a daily schedule that keeps them on track. Most successful people have very similar daily routines. They pray. They read. They exercise. They keep a vision board or a vision book where they post their dreams and goals, and they look at them daily. They speak to their future. Then, creative souls create. Athletes and musicians practice. Inventors build. Whatever you desire to be successful in, create daily goals that will lead you to the picture of success that you see!

WHAT YOU LEARNED ○ DAY 5

Did you learn more about God's Love or God's Plan? Maybe you learned more about His Character or Truth. Place a checkmark in the box next to what you feel you learned about God. Then take a minute to write what you learned.

○ **GOD'S LOVE**

○ **GOD'S CHARACTER**

○ **GOD'S TRUTH**

○ **GOD'S PLAN**

Finish these final steps for today's journal. Checkmark each completed task.

● **HOW DO YOU PLAN TO MAKE THIS A PART OF YOUR EVERY DAY LIFE?**
[Write your answer in the appropriate **MY PLAN** Box in the back of this journal]

● **WHAT IS ONE POTENTIAL AREA OF WEAKNESS YOU WILL ASK THE HOLY SPIRIT TO HELP YOU MAKE STRONGER?**

[Stop now and ask the Holy Spirit for help in this area]

● **ENCOURAGE A FRIEND**
[Share empowering thoughts, ideas, words, and scriptures with your friends. Know what's going on in your friends lives. Make those things a matter of prayer. Find and share scriptures to encourage them.]

THE NAME OF THE FRIEND YOU ENCOURAGED:

THIS IS WHAT I DID: [circle all that you did]

called them   texted them   emailed them   talked to them   wrote a letter

94

MY PERSONAL NOTES

Read the principle and the scriptures below. These are the ideas you want to have strong in your heart. Take your time and think about what you are reading. When you have finished this page, place a checkmark next to DAY 1.

PRINCIPLE
I EXPECT THE BEST OF MYSELF

You always know if you are giving your best. Because you are a great leader that has integrity, you always give your best because that is what you expect of yourself! We don't do our best just to impress others when they are watching. We give one hundred percent when others are looking and when others aren't around, because we know God is always watching. You have an excellent spirit. You have integrity. Because you are a person of great character, you always expect and give your best!

SCRIPTURES
Growing in your knowledge of the Word.

☐ Whoever can be trusted with very little can also be trusted with much, and whoever is dishonest with very little will also be dishonest with much. Luke 16:10 NIV

☐ That is why, for Christ's sake, I delight in weaknesses, in insults, in hardships, in persecutions, in difficulties. For when I am weak, then I am strong. 2 Corinthians 12:10 NIV

☐ I can do all things through Christ who strengthens me. Philippians 4:13 NKJV

Place a check-mark next to the scripture you plan to memorize this week. Once you have recited it to a parent or leader, write the scripture in the appropriate box on your Memorized Word page.

96

STRONGER HEART

For the next three days, you will read the lesson below. For each day you will mark the part of the lesson that stands out to you on that day. Each day requires you to use a different method. When you have completed marking the lesson for that day, checkmark the circle.

○ DAY 2 | <u>Underline</u>   ○ DAY 3 | (Circle)   ○ DAY 4 | [Bracket]

I DO HARD THINGS

You have endurance! You have physical muscles and attitude muscles inside that help you to accomplish even when things get hard. Everyone faces hard things throughout their lives, and you will too. When you come to something that seems difficult or even impossible, you have a choice to make. You can whine and complain about what is hard, and even dread having to deal with it. You can wish the hard thing would disappear and you could choose to just quit. But that's not who you are! You can do all things through Christ! You can conquer anything you set your mind to overcome! And, even when you feel weak and incapable of something, God said that in your weakness, He will give you the strength to walk it out. You have the strength to deal with hard things. You have the ability to conquer the most difficult problems and situations! You are a great leader. You have great endurance. You are full of physical muscles and attitude muscles that will help you win. You are full of confidence and strength and the Spirit of God. No matter what you face, you've got this!

WHAT YOU LEARNED ○ DAY 5

Did you learn more about God's Love or God's Plan? Maybe you learned more about His Character or Truth. Place a checkmark in the box next to what you feel you learned about God. Then take a minute to write what you learned.

○ **GOD'S LOVE**

○ **GOD'S CHARACTER**

○ **GOD'S TRUTH**

○ **GOD'S PLAN**

Finish these final steps for today's journal. Checkmark each completed task.

○ **HOW DO YOU PLAN TO MAKE THIS A PART OF YOUR EVERY DAY LIFE?**
[Write your answer in the appropriate **MY PLAN** Box in the back of this journal]

○ **WHAT IS ONE POTENTIAL AREA OF WEAKNESS YOU WILL ASK THE HOLY SPIRIT TO HELP YOU MAKE STRONGER?**

[Stop now and ask the Holy Spirit for help in this area]

○ **ENCOURAGE A FRIEND**
[Share empowering thoughts, ideas, words, and scriptures with your friends. Know what's going on in your friends lives. Make those things a matter of prayer. Find and share scriptures to encourage them.]

THE NAME OF THE FRIEND YOU ENCOURAGED:

THIS IS WHAT I DID: [circle all that you did]

called them   texted them   emailed them   talked to them   wrote a letter

98

MY PERSONAL NOTES

MEMORIZED WORD

Writing helps you remember. In your weekly entry, you placed a check mark next to the scripture you wanted to memorize. Take a moment and write that scripture in the corresponding week's box below. You can refer back to these pages in the weeks to come as part of your memorization process.

WEEK 1

WEEK 2

WEEK 3

WEEK 4

WEEK 5

WEEK 6

WEEK 7

WEEK 8

WEEK 9

WEEK 10

WEEK 11

WEEK 12

WEEK 13

WEEK 14

WEEK 15

WEEK 16

WEEK 17

WEEK 18

WEEK 19

WEEK 20

WEEK 21

WEEK 22

WEEK 23

WEEK 24

MY PLAN

What is your plan for growth? Every week you are learning more about growing stronger in maturity and engagement. The boxes below correspond with the lessons for each week. Write in what you plan to do to grow stronger from what you have learned. When you have completed this journal, you will have an action plan for growth.

WEEK 1

WEEK 2

WEEK 3

WEEK 4

WEEK 5

WEEK 6

WEEK 7

WEEK 8

WEEK 9

WEEK 10

WEEK 11

WEEK 12

WEEK 13

WEEK 14

105

WEEK 15

WEEK 16

WEEK 17

WEEK 18

WEEK 19

WEEK 20

WEEK 21

WEEK 22

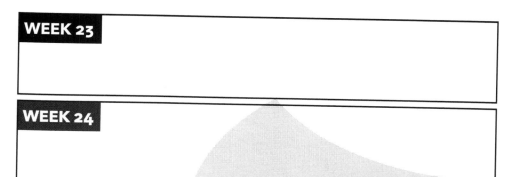

WEEK 23

WEEK 24

WELL DONE! You have finished your journal. You have grown in spiritual maturity and engagement. You are a "Stronger ME!" We hope that these 24 weeks have given you greater confidence, knowledge, wisdom and courage. We believe that God has a great plan for your life. Please accept our prayer as we believe with you for a strong future!

"Father, we ask that you would continue to lead our friend by your Holy Spirit. We are thankful that they have completed this study and that they have opened their heart to You in a greater way. Help them to have clarity and strength to accomplish all you have for them. We are grateful to have offered this resource for them and now ask Your guidance, grace and peace upon their lives. In Jesus name, AMEN!"

107

Made in the USA
Columbia, SC
04 August 2024

39423446R00061